School Projects

SURVIVAL
GUIDES

Studying and Tests

Barbara A. Somervill

Heinemann Library
Chicago, Illinois

© 2009 Heinemann Library
a division of Pearson Inc.
Chicago, Illinois

Customer Service 888-454-2279

Visit our website at www.heinemannlibrary.com

Designed by Richard Parker and Hart McLeod
Colour Reproduction by Dot Gradations Ltd. UK.
Printed and bound in China by Leo Paper Group

13 12 11 10 09
10 9 8 7 6 5 4 3 2 1

Library of Congress Cataloging-in-Publication Data
Somervill, Barbara A.
  Studying and tests / Barbara A. Somervill.
      p. cm. -- (School projects survival guides)
  Includes bibliographical references and index.
  ISBN 978-1-4329-1173-7 (hc) -- ISBN 978-1-4329-1178-2 (pb) 1. Study skills--Juvenile literature. 2. Test-taking skills--Juvenile literature. I. Title.
  LB1049.S677 2008
  378.1'70281--dc22

                          2008001149

Acknowledgments
The author and publishers are grateful to the following for permission to reproduce copyright material: ©Corbis pp. **4**, **16** (Gabe Palmer), **24** (Zefa/Michael A. Keller); ©Getty Images pp. **19** (Blend Images), **27** (Stockbyte); ©Science Photo Library (NASA) p. **10**.

Note paper design features with permission of ©istockphoto.com.

Every effort has been made to contact copyright holders of any material reproduced in this book. Any omissions will be rectified in subsequent printings if notice is given to the publisher.

Disclaimer
All Internet addresses (URLs) given in this book were valid at the time of going to press. However, due to the dynamic nature of the Internet, some addresses may have changed or ceased to exist since publication. While the author and the publishers regret any inconvenience this may cause readers, no responsibility for any such changes can be accepted by either the author or the publishers.

Contents

Some words are printed in bold, **like this**. You can find out what they mean by looking in the glossary.

How You Learn

Get Ready for Success

Step 1: Identify your main learning style.

Step 2: See if you are a verbal or a logical learner.

Step 3: Decide if you like to study alone or with friends.

Lexi is puzzled. She does all of her homework, but when she takes tests, she struggles. She is not sure why, although she does have trouble organizing her study time. She wants to improve her grades, but how?

Seeing, hearing, or doing?

Students learn in many different ways. There is no "right" or "wrong" way. There are three main learning styles: **visual**, **auditory**, and **kinesthetic**. These are fancy names, but they just mean learning by seeing, hearing, and doing.

All learning modes are equally useful. There is no "right" learning style, and no style makes one student smarter than any other. Although everyone has one main learning style, most people use all the styles at least part of the time.

Different students learn in many ways.

Do some research to discover your main learning style. Change how you study according to the way your brain learns new material.

Visual learners learn by seeing. When trying to **memorize** material, they may copy notes, use flashcards, or highlight written material. Visual learners learn easily by reading books, viewing maps or diagrams, or by watching videos or filmstrips.

Auditory learners learn by hearing. It is easy for an auditory learner to follow spoken directions in class or to learn by listening to the teacher. While visual learners like to read to themselves, auditory learners like others to read to them. Students who learn by listening enjoy making up rhymes or jingles to help them study.

Kinesthetic learners learn by doing. They enjoy making models, using their hands, and doing experiments. If a person learns by doing, he or she probably writes notes and lists. If the teacher provides a handout, kinesthetic learners copy key information into a notebook. The act of writing helps them learn.

Ways to Learn Vocabulary

If you learn by seeing...	If you learn by hearing...	If you learn by doing...
• make flashcards for each vocabulary word • read the words and definitions at least three times	• read the list of words aloud, spelling the word and pronouncing each syllable • record the words and definitions on tape and play the tape when you study	• write each spelling word and definition three times • write each word in a sentence, using the correct definition

Other learning styles

When you learn new material, you do not use your entire brain. Different learning styles use different areas of the brain. Besides learning, seeing, and doing, people are also **verbal** or **logical** learners. Further, people can also be **social** or **solitary** learners. A verbal learner gains knowledge by using words. Logical learners learn through reason or relating to patterns, such as those used in math.

Verbal learners depend on reading, writing, and working with words. Most verbal learners enjoy clever rhymes, tongue twisters, and funny stories. They can better learn key ideas by relating them to a song or theme.

Logical learners depend on drawings, diagrams, patterns, and graphs to help them learn. They are usually good at math and science because those subjects use numbers, measurements, charts, and diagrams. Logical learners make lists to keep themselves on track. They may also enjoy brainteasers, riddles, and mysteries.

A PUZZLER

Exercise your mind. The following letters represent a series of words you learned as a young child. Do you see a pattern? Read the letters aloud. What do you hear? Use your most comfortable learning style to figure out the answer.

O T T F F S _ _ _ _

The answer appears on page 32.

Social and solitary learners

Do you learn better in a group or by yourself? Social learners are group people. They prefer to study and learn in a group. They enjoy team sports and projects and playing games with others. As a social learner, you might work well with a study buddy with whom you can do homework or study for a test.

Solitary learners like to learn and study by themselves. Solitary learners would rather read alone, set their own goals, and work independently. If you are a solitary learner, you might enjoy keeping a learning log. This is a journal in which you record what you read and study, ideas for projects, or daily writing.

Combined learning styles

When you study or learn, you are only using a small part of your brain. Each learning style uses a different brain section. You can improve your success by exercising your brain in the same way you might exercise your muscles.

The more you work your mind, the easier it is to learn. Do puzzles, make models, or create jingles about math rules. Although you have one main learning style, you can expand your mind by working with other styles. Study by seeing, hearing, and doing. Your "stronger" brain will help you succeed.

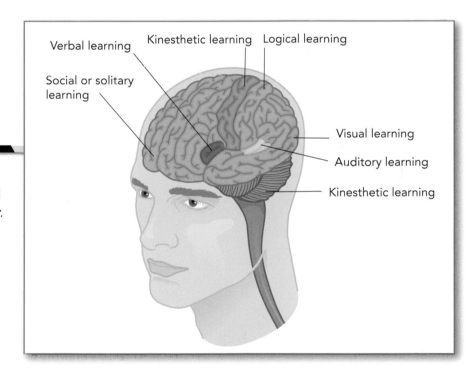

Use more parts of your brain and build your learning power.

✓ I understand that people learn in different ways.
✓ I know whether I work better in groups or alone.
✓ I use my most comfortable learning style.

Planning for Studying

What a week! Lexi has soccer practice twice, a piano lesson, a spelling test, daily homework, and a written report due on Friday. Before she gets behind in her work, she makes a study schedule. She also allows for some free time every day.

Scheduling study time

Adults with busy lives keep a calendar handy to schedule meetings and activities. As a busy student, you should do the same thing. In an average week, you have homework, tests, sports, and other activities. You also need time with your family and friends.

One way to get everything done is to use a study calendar. Keep track of when assignments are due. Break large tasks into smaller units and enter each unit on the calendar. This will help you balance school, family, and outside activities.

Get Ready for Success

Step 1: Set up a study schedule.

Step 2: Work in a quiet area.

Step 3: Plan computer time.

Make a study schedule that allows you enough time to get everything done. Here is an example:

	Monday	Tuesday	Wednesday	Thursday	Friday
3:30-4:30	Homework	Homework	Piano lesson	Homework	Reading
4:30-5:30	Writing report	Soccer practice	Studying for math test	Studying for math test	Soccer practice
5:30-6:30	Chores and dinner	Chores and dinner	Chores and dinner	Chores and dinner	Chores and dinner
6:30 on	Piano practice / Free time	Writing report / Free time	Report artwork / Free time	Final report copy / Free time	Free time

Setting up a study center

If you are like most people your age, you probably do your homework in front of the television or with music blasting. That is not a good way to study. Although it may take some adjustment, you should work in a quiet, calm place. Study time is more effective when you work in a peaceful study center.

Set up a study center with a desk or table at a comfortable height for writing. Keep a full set of supplies on hand while you work. You should have a calculator, a dictionary, paper, pens and pencils, a ruler, schoolbooks, note cards, and a watch or clock. If you are an auditory learner, use a computer or other method to record any study information, such as spelling words or lists of dates.

Avoid television, radio, or other interruptions while you work. This includes phone time. During the week, limit your phone chats to after your work is done.

Planning a computer work station

Not everyone has a home computer, but if you do, you need to make the area study-friendly. You may need to share a computer with other family members. If so, talk with the family and set up regular computer time. When you have scheduled computer time, put it to good use. Switch off the instant messenger and do your work!

If you set up a study center and plan your study time in advance, it will be much easier for you to get everything done. Making good use of your study time will also help you balance schoolwork and other activities.

CHAPTER CHECKLIST

✓ I set up a work schedule.
✓ I have a quiet place for studying.
✓ I planned computer time.

Getting the Best from Books

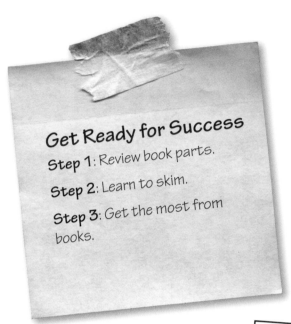

Get Ready for Success

Step 1: Review book parts.

Step 2: Learn to skim.

Step 3: Get the most from books.

Lexi uses books in class, in the library, and for reports. Her teacher explains that today's textbooks are loaded with helpful clues to aid learning. He shows the class how to use the different parts of a textbook to be more successful.

Text clues

Open your science book. What do you see? As you skim through the pages, you should find **headings**, **subheads**, pictures, diagrams, charts and graphs, and **captions**. The book will have a table of contents, an index, and a glossary. The way the book presents information is designed to help you learn.

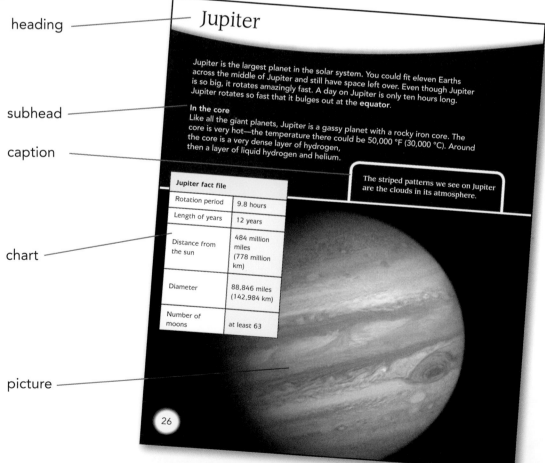

heading —— Jupiter

Jupiter is the largest planet in the solar system. You could fit eleven Earths across the middle of Jupiter and still have space left over. Even though Jupiter is so big, it rotates amazingly fast. A day on Jupiter is only ten hours long. Jupiter rotates so fast that it bulges out at the **equator**.

subhead —— **In the core**
Like all the giant planets, Jupiter is a gassy planet with a rocky iron core. The core is very hot—the temperature there could be 50,000 °F (30,000 °C). Around the core is a very dense layer of hydrogen, then a layer of liquid hydrogen and helium.

caption ——

The striped patterns we see on Jupiter are the clouds in its atmosphere.

chart ——

Jupiter fact file	
Rotation period	9.8 hours
Length of years	12 years
Distance from the sun	484 million miles (778 million km)
Diameter	88,846 miles (142,984 km)
Number of moons	at least 63

picture ——

26

HELPFUL HINT!

Skimming—quick reading—does not take the place of reading more carefully. It helps you prepare for what you will read.

Today's assignment is to read a chapter about the solar system. Take a peek at what you will learn. The headings announce major sections of the chapter. Subheads refer to topics under a heading. By scanning the pages, you can predict the information you will read. If you are a kinesthetic learner, take notes of key headings and subheads as you skim the pages. For auditory learners, say the headings and subheads aloud.

HELPFUL HINT!

Spend at least 20 minutes reading every day. It does not matter what you read. Just open a book and do it! You will learn new vocabulary, improve your reading skills, and improve your own writing skills.

Pictures, captions, graphic materials

The chapter you read has an illustration of the solar system. Look at the picture and think about what you see. First, you notice the planets' order from the sun. Next, you see that some of the planets are larger than others. Read the caption below the picture. As you review the picture, take notes about what you see. As you read the chapter, you will find that the illustration supports the text. The book features provide the same information in different ways.

Sometimes it is difficult to understand a collection of facts and figures written in paragraph form. A map, chart, or graph can explain the same material in **graphic** form. A paragraph about the distances between the sun and various planets may be difficult to understand. A graph or map of the solar system that includes the distances makes it easier to understand distance.

Use graphic items as learning tools. If you are a visual learner, pictures and diagrams make learning easy. For auditory learners, describe what you see out loud. Kinesthetic learners might take notes or copy the graphic materials into a notebook.

Finding key facts

An important part of learning is finding the key facts. As you read a paragraph, look for the main idea. What facts support the main idea? You might use a **graphic organizer** to record key facts for studying later. Writing a graphic organizer helps kinesthetic learners, while reading one helps visual learners. Read the following paragraph and note the main idea and supporting facts.

> Jupiter, the largest planet, has four large moons and dozens of smaller ones. In 1610, the Italian scientist Galileo first discovered Jupiter's largest moons. Galileo named the moons Io, Europa, Ganymede, and Callisto.

You might use a main idea graphic organizer to take notes from a textbook or nonfiction book. Here is an example:

Main idea: Jupiter has many moons	Fact: 4 large moons, dozens of small ones
	Fact: Galileo discovered four large moons in 1610
	Fact: The largest moons are named Io, Europa, Ganymede, and Callisto

HELPFUL HINT!

If you learn by listening, try using **mnemonics** to memorize. A mnemonic, pronounced nem-AH-nik, is a short rhyme or phrase that aids the memory. For example, _My very educated mother just served us noodles_ is a mnemonic for the names of the planets in their order from the sun.

There is a hidden saying in these letters. Can you find it? Train your eyes to look for patterns of letters that are familiar and stretch your verbal learning skills. Cross out letters that do not belong to reveal the message.

GPYOULAQTECANASTCATCHKEDFQZMORERYOPFLIESKUJQFG

MGUFTWITHMUHONEYWTEBTHANMUSWITHVESLVINEGARNPL

The answer appears on page 32.

Context clues

As you read, you will come across unfamiliar words. Many of these words will appear in the glossary at the back of the book. A glossary is simply a dictionary of certain words used in the book you are reading.

Understanding key vocabulary is important. If you do not understand the vocabulary, you might not fully understand what you are learning. You may figure out the meaning of words through **context clues**, much like solving a puzzle. Here is an example. Sam is *tenacious*, but his sister gives up on projects easily. What does *tenacious* mean? Sam is the opposite of his sister, who gives up easily. Therefore, he is firm and determined to succeed, which is the meaning of tenacious.

Reading unfamiliar words, phrases, or difficult sentences aloud helps bring out the meaning. Copy the words into a learning log. Learn vocabulary by seeing it, hearing it, or writing it. Refer back to the chart on page 5 to see how these methods will make learning easier.

CHAPTER CHECKLIST

✓ I read for key facts.
✓ I take notes as I read.
✓ I look for context clues to help with hard words.

Learning from Other Sources

Get Ready for Success

Step 1: Improve listening skills.

Step 2: Use homework and handouts as study guides.

Step 3: Go online for homework help.

Lexi has homework pages and notes from class to sort through. She is getting ready to study for a test. Lexi puts the pages in order with oldest first and most recent pages last, and then numbers each page. As she studies, she reviews the material in the order it was taught in class.

Improve listening skills

You can train yourself to develop better listening skills. Make a set of 5 W's and 1 H charts. These charts cover who, what, when, where, why, and how. Each night spend ten minutes watching a news broadcast. After a story is over, test yourself on what you heard. Fill in the sections of the organizer.

Once you have mastered a news report, test yourself on something bigger. Listen to a chapter of a book on tape, and then fill in the same organizer. You can apply your new listening skills by paying closer attention in class.

Use a 5 W's and 1 H graphic organizer to test your listening skills.

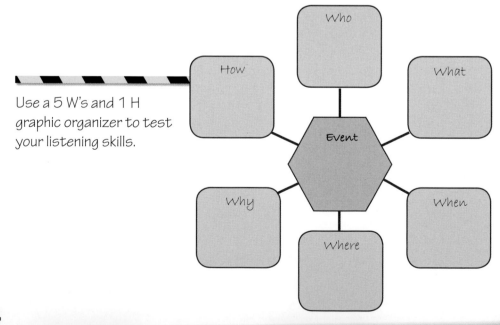

Class notes, homework, and handouts

Review your notes with a highlighter or marking pen in your hand. When you come to an important fact, highlight or star it. Use a different color marker or code to note information that is hard to understand. The different marking will remind you to review that material more than once.

Use old homework the same way. Begin by rereading the questions asked. Try working out the answer in your mind. Double-check your mental work with the answer you wrote on your homework paper. Rework questions or problems that seemed difficult when the work was first done.

Going online

Online study aids include **search engines**, programs to create flashcards, homework helper sites, math and language games, and puzzles. Online study aids can help you look at a subject from a new and different angle. You may find a new way to explain a difficult concept or practice exercises to test your knowledge.

What are you watching?

Depending on what you watch, television can also be a learning tool. If your class is studying about volcanoes, look for a show on that topic. You may find something in the daily listings, or you might find a DVD or video at the library.

Regardless of your learning style, keep a pad and pencil by your side and take notes. Learning does not always come from a book. If you develop skills that help you use and learn from other sources, you will enjoy greater success in your education.

CHAPTER CHECKLIST

✓ I organized notes and handouts.
✓ I found online study help.
✓ I took notes.

Different Types of Tests

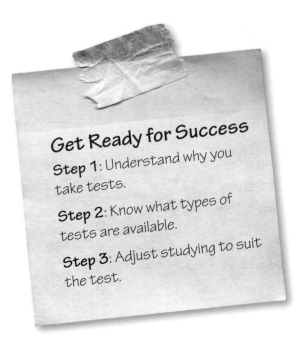

Get Ready for Success

Step 1: Understand why you take tests.

Step 2: Know what types of tests are available.

Step 3: Adjust studying to suit the test.

It is time to put your studying to work. Studying equals learning. Some material is learned for a test, while other material is learned as homework. Sometimes studying lets you learn new facts, ideas, or skills. Do not think you are wasting your time if you learn something that is not tested. Everything you learn has a use and a purpose.

Why tests?

Oh, no! There's another test on Friday! You might wonder why you have to take so many tests. The reasons behind testing are not to scare or punish you. Tests do several different jobs.

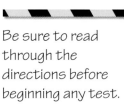

Be sure to read through the directions before beginning any test.

First of all, tests help your teacher find out if a lesson has been successful. If too many students perform badly on a test, something is wrong. The teacher may need to reteach the material in a different way.

Tests also support learning. They highlight the information being tested, which reminds students about important facts. You should look at a test as an opportunity for success. If you study and know the material, you will do well.

HELPFUL HINT!

Write down key notes and facts on the back of the test. Note math formulas, key dates or events, science facts, or other key information that will help you take your test.

Types of tests

Success in testing goes back to how you learn. If you are a verbal learner, you might find taking an essay test easier than a logical learner would. Logical and visual learners might do better on a test that requires reading graphs or charts. No matter how you learn, you can improve your chances of success if you develop test-taking skills.

True/false

A true/false test presents statements and asks you to figure out if the statement is true or not. When you take a true/false test, look out for words that make the statement either all positive or all negative. Underline words such as all, always, every, everyone, none, never, or no one. Think carefully about whether the statement could possibly be true before answering these questions.

Multiple choice

A multiple choice test presents several possible answers to a question. You must choose the correct answer. Read the question carefully. You might be asked which word does not have the same meaning rather than to find a **synonym**. Review the choices and cross off answers you know are wrong. Then, pick the answer you believe is correct.

Fill-in the blank

A fill-in the blank test gives a statement with some information missing. You must provide the correct information. Read the sentence to yourself and see if you know the word that goes in the blank. Use context clues to help figure out the answer. For instance, _____ wrote the *The Lion, The Witch, and the Wardrobe*. The question is asking for a person's name.

Short answer and essay questions

Short answer and essay question tests ask you to write your answers in full sentences. A short answer is usually one to four sentences. An essay response may be several paragraphs. Read the entire question and think about your answer. Underline the key elements of the question. Do you need to tell three ways something happens or why a date in history is important? You might make a short list of key items you wish to include in your answer in the margin. Allow yourself plenty of time to write your answer.

HELPFUL HINT!

When answering an essay or short answer question, begin your answer by rewording the question. The question reads, Name two of Jupiter's moons. Your answer should say, Two of Jupiter's moons are Io and Callisto.

Standardized tests

In addition to tests given by your teacher you may have to also take **standardized** tests. Standardized tests are given in many schools and on many subjects. They may include true/false, multiple choice, or other types of questions that are answered on a specially designed answer sheet. These tests usually cover math and reading skills. They are given to find out what students know at a certain age. You cannot study for these tests, but you can prepare. Have a good night's rest and eat a good breakfast. Take your time during the test, reading all directions fully before answering.

A standardized test is different in format from a regular test.

Memorizing or reasoning

You will take many tests that require you to memorize material. Such tests include spelling words and definitions, history dates, and math formulas. Flashcards work well for items that need to be memorized. Mnemonics or jingles will also work for memorizing. True/false, multiple choice, matching, and fill-in the blank tests usually require you to recall an answer from memory.

Some tests require **reasoning**, such as figuring out an answer or drawing a conclusion. In a science test, you might need to explain why or how something happens. A math word problem also requires reasoning. Short answer and essay questions usually need an answer that you reason out.

CHAPTER CHECKLIST

✓ I understand the types of tests.
✓ I can answer an essay question.
✓ I know how to memorize for testing.

Studying and Preparing for a Test

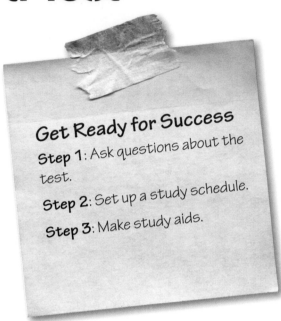

Get Ready for Success

Step 1: Ask questions about the test.

Step 2: Set up a study schedule.

Step 3: Make study aids.

Lexi is having a test in science—her worst subject. She knows she learns best when she hears the material. She takes a positive approach and makes a tape of everything on the study sheet, including vocabulary words, spellings, and definitions. She uses a main ideas graphic organizer to sort key information.

Know what to study

Knowing what to study for a test is one of the biggest problems students face. Some teachers hand out review sheets. Others tell students to review their notes or to study a particular chapter. If you are not sure what the test will cover, ask!

Is the test multiple choice, fill-in the blank, or some other format? What specific material is covered? If the answer is "Chapter 4," then review that chapter. As you review take notes, make flashcards, or make a tape of key words and facts. Check your spelling on every word in your notes.

Some students study well with a study buddy. If you are a social learner, set up time for you and a friend to study together. Plan your review session, including several different learning methods. Ask each other questions, use flashcards, and read notes aloud to each other.

If you would rather study alone, make a plan. First, review all your notes. Write a list of key words, dates, and facts, and then copy it a second time. Make a list of questions you might ask if you were giving the test—then answer them. Review all questions in your textbook or on handouts from the teacher.

Do the worst first! If there is a subject you like less than others you are studying, do the work for that subject first. After that, your work will move along quickly.

Scheduling study time

Spread out your studying throughout the week in order to avoid doing it all the night before the test. Make studying your main concern. There are dozens of excuses for not studying for Friday's test on Monday. Put those excuses aside and start studying. The more frequently you review the material, the more likely you will remember information needed for the test. Early studying also allows you to identify problem areas and get help before test day.

Make a schedule and stick to it. You do not need to study three hours every night for a week. In fact, studying that long may not help. Your brain gets muddled, and you forget what you reviewed. Spread studying out over the week—give your brain a chance to work out.

Make a study schedule that allows you to get all of your studying done before a test. Here is an example:

Monday	Tuesday	Wednesday	Thursday	Friday
30 minutes	30 minutes	45 minutes	45 minutes	15 minutes
Review all notes, homework, handouts	Review classroom textbook	Make lists of key questions, vocabulary, facts	Review all materials	Skim over difficult areas before school

Create study aids

The advantage of making your own study aids is that you learn while you make them. Think about it. You learn by hearing, so you make a tape of key dates in a history lesson. You learn those dates as you make the tape.

If you learn by seeing, flashcards, graphic organizers, color-coding or highlighting, and diagrams will help you study. If you learn by hearing, use recordings, music, poems, rhymes, and mnemonics. For kinesthetic learners, making flashcards helps you more than reading them. You can also study by making graphic organizers, writing lists, or coloring sections on a diagram or illustration.

HELPFUL HINT!

Review all materials *before* you make study aids. Then, figure out what materials will provide the most help to learn what you need to know.

Study processes

Reading success comes from following a process. Three of these reading processes also work well for studying. They are R-T-C, SQ3R, and SMRR.

R-T-C (Read-Test-Check) works for visual and kinesthetic learners. Read the material. Write notes about what you read. Test yourself and check your answers. R-T-C works alone or with a friend.

SQ3R (Survey, Question, Read, Recite, Review) is excellent if you learn by seeing or hearing. Begin by previewing the text for key ideas. As you do so, ask yourself questions you want answered in your reading. Then, read the material and recite a quick summary of what you read. Finally, review to make sure you understand key facts.

In SMRR (Skim, Mark, Read, and Reread) you skim the material and mark key elements with a highlighter. A word of caution—do not highlight in schoolbooks. Look for the main topic and supporting facts. Now read and reread the material to make sure you understand the material.

This puzzler helps you understand why it is important to look beyond the obvious when you study. How many squares do you see? Copy or trace this diagram onto a sheet of paper. Then use different colored highlighters to mark the squares.

The answer appears on page 32.

Ask for help

After you have studied, you may find there is something you still do not understand. Now is the time to ask for help. You can ask a teacher, parent, or classmate to explain the material to you. Be sure you understand all the material before the test.

CHAPTER CHECKLIST

✓ I planned my studying.
✓ I made study aids.
✓ I asked for the help I need.

Test Day

Get Ready for Success

Step 1: Get plenty of rest.

Step 2: Review your notes.

Step 3: Relax!

Lexi is nervous, but she eats a good breakfast before school. Before she leaves home, she checks her backpack for pencils, a ruler, and her notes. Those are supplies she needs to take the test. She makes a quick review of her notes, and then leaves for school.

Dealing with nerves

Everyone is nervous before taking a big test. It is perfectly normal. Try to have a good night's sleep before the test. You will do better if you are well rested. Eat breakfast. Your body and brain need fuel every day, and test day is no exception.

A good breakfast sets you up for a successful school day.

If you have done your studying in advance, take it easy. You have done everything you could. Now, take a few deep breaths and relax. Picture yourself getting a good grade. Success on a test comes from studying and confidence. If you have done the first part, you should be confident of a positive result.

Read directions

You might be surprised to learn how many low grades come from not reading the directions. Check the board to see if your teacher has written any new or different directions. Read all the directions. Here is a problem that happens quite often. You see the test is true/false, so you do not bother to read the directions. You enter T or F on each blank. Unfortunately, the directions call for using + or 0, not T or F.

Make the following actions a test-taking habit. When you receive your test, write your name on the appropriate line. Scan the test to see how many questions there are, what types of questions, and what directions you must follow. Read the directions for each section, underlining key phrases. Go to the top of the page and begin taking your test. These actions should only take three minutes, but they will help you do well.

Do not cheat

Every student comes across test questions for which they do not know the answer. When this happens to you, do not cheat and look on your neighbor's paper. Your neighbor may not know the correct answer either. Do your own work and succeed on what you know. You will feel better about yourself and your grade if you earn it yourself.

Test-taking strategies

Your teacher will not mark you down for guessing. If you are taking a multiple choice, true/false, matching, or fill-in test, guessing is a good idea. Wait until you have finished all the other questions before making your guesses. There may be some information in another question that will help you find the correct answer.

Making choices

Whenever a test offers choices, cross off answers you know cannot be right. What do you have left? Reword the question into a statement with a blank. Read the statement using the remaining possible choices. The question asks which planet is closest to the sun. You reword the question to read, "Venus is closest to the sun," and then "Mercury is closest to the sun." The mention of Mercury triggers your memory. You have the right answer.

HELPFUL HINT!

When taking a test where you fill in circles for the answers, keep a highlighter on your desk. When you have to skip a question, highlight the number. This will help you keep track of question and answer numbers.

True/false tests work the same way. If you do not know the answer, rework the statement keeping the same meaning. The statement reads: *Mars is closer to the sun than the Earth*. Is this true or false? If you are not sure, rework the statement to what you know is true. *The planets in the order from the sun are Mercury, Venus, Earth, Mars, and so on*. Mars is *not* closer to the sun than the Earth. The statement is false.

For essay-style tests, look carefully at the question. If you must include three examples in your answer, write 1., 2., and 3. in the margin. Write a key word next to each number to represent each example. As you write your essay answer, cross off the examples as they are used.

Don't know the answer?

It is possible that you may not know the answer to a question. If so, skip this question and move on. Before you do so, circle the number to remind yourself to go back to this particular question. If you waste too much time trying to come up with an answer for one question, you may not finish the entire test.

After you finish the test, go back to answer questions you skipped. Try to figure out the answer, but do not get upset if there is one question you simply cannot answer.

Keep an eye on the clock so that you use your time well during a test.

Budgeting time

Before the test begins, ask your teacher how much time you have to take the test. Look at the clock and note the start time in the corner of your test paper. Based on the time available, you need to figure out how much time you can spend on each section of the test.

Based on a 30-minute test, here is a typical time budget. Allow three minutes to review the test and directions. Use 20 to 22 minutes to take the test. Use the remaining time to check over your work. However you budget your time, keep your eye on the clock. You do not want to run out of time before you finish the test.

What did you learn?

If you had to take a test on the alphabet today, you would say, "No problem!" You know that material, so you feel comfortable being tested on it. That is the key to every test you will ever take—know the material. If you study and learn the material, you cannot help but succeed.

CHAPTER CHECKLIST

✓ I control my nerves.
✓ I follow all directions.
✓ I will be a success.

Study Aids

There are many study aids that you can make to help organize and learn information.

Timeline

When studying with a timeline, you can use the timeline two ways. Begin by putting dates in every box from your notes. Then, after studying, fill in the matching events as a "self test." You can also use this organizer to test your knowledge of dates. Write in the events from your notes. After studying, close your books and add the dates.

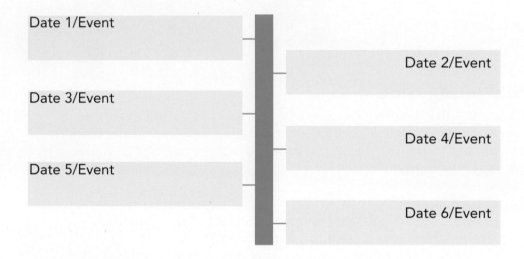

Date 1/Event

Date 2/Event

Date 3/Event

Date 4/Event

Date 5/Event

Date 6/Event

Main Idea

For studying, fill in the main idea box as you study. After you have finished reviewing the material, close your book and fill in the supporting fact boxes.

	Fact:
Main idea:	Fact:
	Fact:

Word Web

Word webs are excellent study tools for learning vocabulary. These organizers can be used in any subject where you are learning new words and their use.

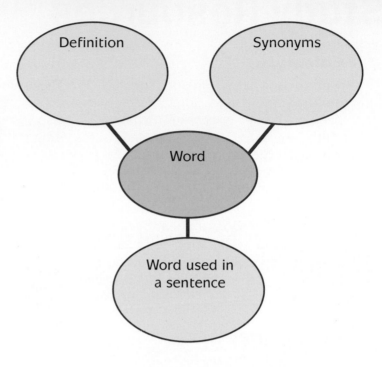

5 W's and 1 H

As a study guide, fill in the central box with an event. After you have studied, close your notes and fill in the remaining boxes from memory.

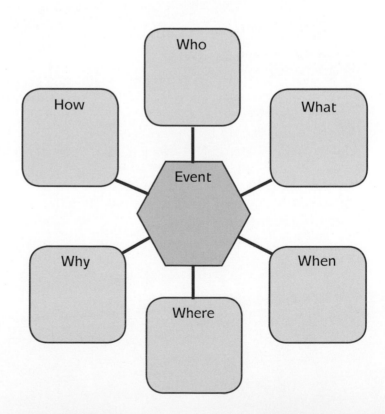

Study Resources

Calculator

A calculator helps you add, subtract, multiply, and divide. Some calculators perform higher or more difficult math functions. Using a calculator depends on class rules. If your teacher does not allow you to use a calculator in class, then you should only use one on homework to check your answers. Do not cheat because you will only be cheating yourself. If you need to divide in your head on a test, you need to practice *without* the calculator at home.

Dictionaries

Most dictionaries do more than just tell definitions of words. Standard dictionaries may contain synonyms, antonyms, usage, word origin, and pronunciation. There are also biographical and geographical dictionaries.

Thesaurus

A thesaurus provides synonyms and antonyms. Warning! Not every synonym has the exact same meaning. Dollar, euro, and pound are all types of money, but they are not identical in meaning.

Homework Help

There are many sites that offer help with homework. HomeworkSpot.com also offers suggestions on science projects, staying healthy, and arts and crafts, among other topics.

Internet Public Library

The Internet Public Library (www.ipl.org) is like having a library on your desktop computer. You can search through the site for information on social studies, science, medicine, literature, and so on. You can read a book, a magazine, or a newspaper.

Search Engines

Search engines have many interesting names—Ask.com, Google, and Yahoo, to name a few. Each of these search engines works in the same way. Enter a topic in the search window, click, and the engine finds articles and websites that fill your request. Be patient. You may not find what you need on the first attempt.

Glossary

auditory relating to the sense of hearing

caption short description of a picture, graph, chart, or other illustration

context clue clue to the meaning of a word that is found in the sentence or phrase in which the word appears

graphic picture, graph, chart, map, illustration, or drawn element

graphic organizer method of arranging information in a visual manner

heading main division into which a document is divided

kinesthetic having to do with the sense of touch, doing, or hands-on activity

logical based on facts, reason, or clear thinking

memorize commit something to your memory, to learn by heart

mnemonic rhyme, phrase, or jingle designed to help you remember

reasoning process of using logical thinking to find results or draw conclusions

search engine program on the Internet designed to find articles and websites on specific topics

social relating to people in groups and how they work with each other

solitary preferring to be alone

standardized test administered to a large group of students in order to compare the knowledge of those students

synonym word with the same or similar meaning, such as home and house

subhead secondary heading or subtopic

verbal relating to words, both spoken and written

visual relating to vision or sight, something that is seen

Index

Puzzler Answers

Page 6: S E N T. The letters stand for One, Two, Three, Four, Five, Six, Seven, Eight, Nine, Ten.

Page 13: You can catch more flies with honey than with vinegar.

Page 23: There are 14 squares. Each small square= 9, the entire diagram=1 square, and there are 4 medium-sized squares composed of 4 squares each.

NO. **002**

FROM: _____

DATE: _____

☐ *to share*
☐ *to keep*

this book belongs to:

PLEASE RETURN TO OWNER IF BORROWED OR FOUND

THE WORLD NEEDS

Who You Were Made to Be

JOANNA GAINES

ILLUSTRATED BY JULIANNA SWANEY

An Imprint of Thomas Nelson
thomasnelson.com

I hope that you know and love who you are
for all of the beautiful and unique and magical
gifts you have to offer to the world.

May you always look at life with your eyes wide
open. Be quick to learn from others and see and
celebrate the differences in all of humanity.
Be kind to others and to yourself.

And may you always believe that the
world needs who you were made to be.

LOVE, Joanna

Today is the day for the ride of our lives,

when a confetti of color will fill up the sky!

Plenty of pink, a bounty of blue,
and orange, green, and yellow too!

We all play a part, both me and you,

as we build our very own hot-air balloons!

We'll gather supplies and make them our own
and prepare to take flight into the great unknown.

It doesn't take us long to see . . .

that we all work so very differently.

Some of us work alone.

And some of us
work side by side.

Some of us are
quiet and like to think
things through.

And others prefer to chitchat
about all we have to do!

Some of us think through every possibility before we jump in.

And some of us know what we
like before we even begin.

Sometimes we're scientific
and rely on our smarts.

Sometimes we're creative
and lean into the arts.

Some of us are resourceful.

We like to work with whatever's on hand.

And some of us are extravagant.

We like to go big whenever we can!

Some of us are teachers
and share what we know.

But all of us are learners.

Together is how we grow!

So, by now you can
probably see . . .

how we all work so
very differently.

We've done our very best,

and now it's time to fly.

See how beautiful it can be when

our differences share the same sky?

We may not look
or work or think the same,

but we all have an
important part to play.

All of us can be kind,
compassionate, and gracious.

All of us can be helpful,

considerate, and courageous.

So remember who you are.

This is your life to live.

Don't ever hold back.

You have so much to give!

You're one of a kind,

and it's so clear to see:

The world needs
who YOU were made to be.

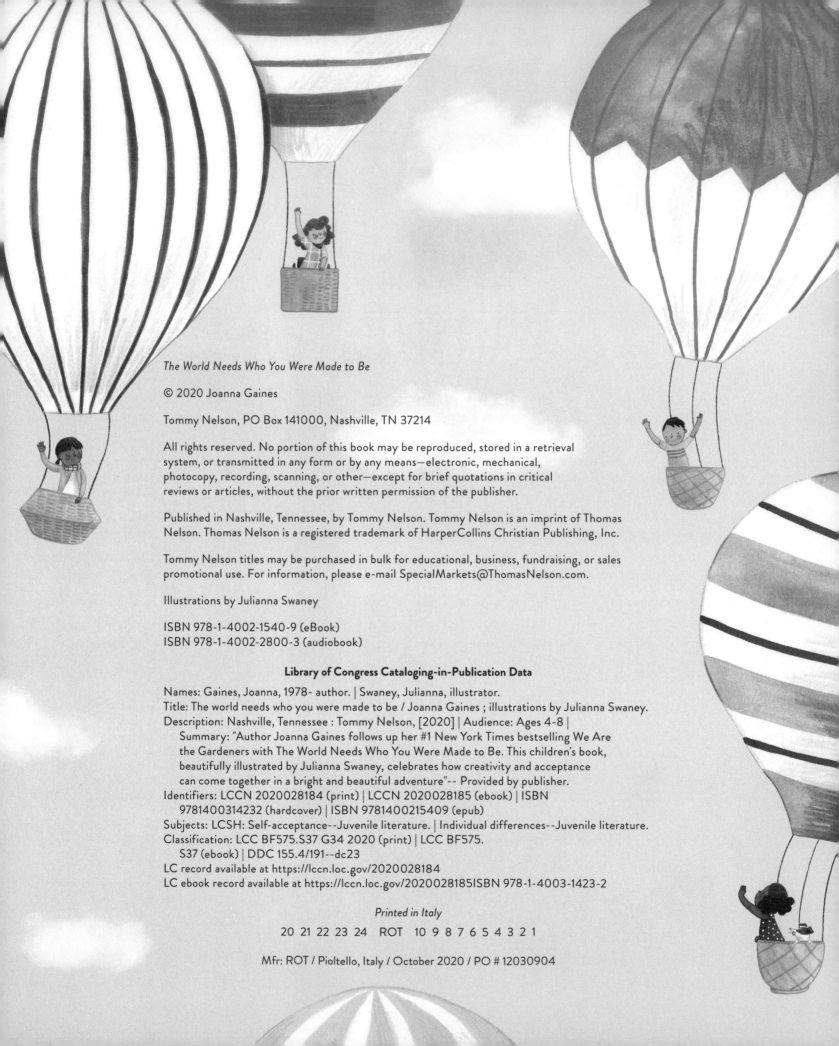

The World Needs Who You Were Made to Be

© 2020 Joanna Gaines

Tommy Nelson, PO Box 141000, Nashville, TN 37214

Published in Nashville, Tennessee, by Tommy Nelson. Tommy Nelson is an imprint of Thomas Nelson. Thomas Nelson is a registered trademark of HarperCollins Christian Publishing, Inc.

Tommy Nelson titles may be purchased in bulk for educational, business, fundraising, or sales promotional use. For information, please e-mail SpecialMarkets@ThomasNelson.com.

Illustrations by Julianna Swaney

ISBN 978-1-4002-1540-9 (eBook)
ISBN 978-1-4002-2800-3 (audiobook)

Library of Congress Cataloging-in-Publication Data

Names: Gaines, Joanna, 1978- author. | Swaney, Julianna, illustrator.
Title: The world needs who you were made to be / Joanna Gaines ; illustrations by Julianna Swaney.
Description: Nashville, Tennessee : Tommy Nelson, [2020] | Audience: Ages 4-8 |
    Summary: "Author Joanna Gaines follows up her #1 New York Times bestselling We Are the Gardeners with The World Needs Who You Were Made to Be. This children's book, beautifully illustrated by Julianna Swaney, celebrates how creativity and acceptance can come together in a bright and beautiful adventure"-- Provided by publisher.
Identifiers: LCCN 2020028184 (print) | LCCN 2020028185 (ebook) | ISBN 9781400314232 (hardcover) | ISBN 9781400215409 (epub)
Subjects: LCSH: Self-acceptance--Juvenile literature. | Individual differences--Juvenile literature.
Classification: LCC BF575.S37 G34 2020 (print) | LCC BF575.S37 (ebook) | DDC 155.4/191--dc23
LC record available at https://lccn.loc.gov/2020028184
LC ebook record available at https://lccn.loc.gov/2020028185ISBN 978-1-4003-1423-2

Printed in Italy

20 21 22 23 24 ROT 10 9 8 7 6 5 4 3 2 1

Mfr: ROT / Pioltello, Italy / October 2020 / PO # 12030904

12'8"

yellow + white

pink stripes

Swan basket

4'2"

PANELS

SKIRT

BASKET

gate

3'5"

light green under

blue + green

alternating Colors

Painted green

CABLES

over-under

weaving a basket

sand bags

Painted design

alternating Colors

alternating Colors

NET

FIN

PROPELLER

PULLY

light green under

GONDOLA

dark pink or orange

ENVELOPE

PANELS

SKIRT

BASKET

12'8"

8'8"

stripes

gate

3'5"

Swan basket

4'2"

over-under

Painted design

BASKET

Painted green

alternating lors